Blockchain: What It Is And How It Could Change Our Lives

The Hidden Economy Revealed

Lawrence C. Martini

© Copyright 2016 - All rights reserved.

In no way is it legal to reproduce, duplicate, or transmit any part of this document in either electronic means or in printed format. Recording of this publication is strictly prohibited and any storage of this document is not allowed unless with written permission from the publisher. All rights reserved.

The information provided herein is stated to be truthful and consistent, in that any liability, in terms of inattention or otherwise, by any usage or abuse of any policies, processes, or directions contained within is the solitary and utter responsibility of the recipient reader. Under no circumstances will any legal responsibility or blame be held against the publisher for any reparation, damages, or monetary loss due to the information herein, either directly or indirectly.

Respective authors own all copyrights not held by the publisher.

Legal Notice:

This book is copyright protected. This is only for personal use. You cannot amend, distribute, sell, use, quote or paraphrase any part or the content within this book without the consent of the author or copyright owner. Legal action will be pursued if this is breached.

Disclaimer Notice:

Please note the information contained within this document is for educational and entertainment purposes only. Every attempt has been made to provide accurate, up to date and reliable complete information. No warranties of any kind are expressed or implied. Readers acknowledge that the author is not engaging in the rendering of legal, financial, medical or professional advice.

By reading this document, the reader agrees that under no circumstances are we responsible for any losses, direct or indirect, which are incurred as a result of the use of information contained within this document, including, but not limited to, —errors, omissions, or inaccuracies.

Table of Contents

Introduction 5

Chapter 1 - What is Blockchain? 8

Chapter 2 - How Blockchain Works 21

Chapter 3 - Blockchains and Internet of Things 47

Chapter 4 - Blockchains and Cryptocurrencies 60

Chapter 5 - Ethereum Investment Opportunities 73

Chapter 6 - Smart Contracts: Their Impact in Real Life 83

Chapter 7 - Examples of Blockchains Applications 95

Chapter 8 - Future Developments in Big Financial Industries 101

Conclusion 107

Introduction

This book serves as an introductory guide about blockchain and how it is gradually disrupting industries, especially the financial world.

The World Wide Web connects billions of people around the world, and it is awesome in doing its role for communication and collaboration. But because the Internet is designed for moving and storing information and not actual value, it has affected minimal change in how we do business.

If you send someone data contained in an email in the form of a jpg, ppt, or pdf, you are just sending a copy of the data and not the original. And depending on the rights granted to the people who received the copies, they can make copies and share them as well.

But you can't do this with money. You can't just print it and use it to buy services. So despite of the powerful role of Internet, we still have to depend on intermediaries to establish trust. Governments, banks, and even online companies such as Google and Facebook are working to establish our identity as well as ownership of assets.

And here comes blockchain – the first electronic medium for value exchange between peers. The protocol of blockchain sets the rules – in form of worldwide distribution of computations and cryptology, which makes certain that the integrity of data is exchanged among billions of devices without the need to pass through an external party. You will learn how trust is encoded in the blockchain platform after you read this book.

You may not have felt it yet, but blockchain is gradually changing our lives. Experts project that this technology can be disruptive enough that it will lead to a revolution that will alter the industries and create new ones in the generations to come.

Chapter 1 - What is Blockchain?

Blockchain refers to the public ledger where all Bitcoin transactions are recorded. It is continuously growing as 'completed' blocks are being added to the ledger as new transactions occur. Blocks are added to the blockchain in a chronological and linear order. Every node (the computer linked to the BTC network) will receive a copy of the blockchain that gets automatically downloaded upon linking in the network. The blockchain contains complete details about the addresses as well as their balances right from the original block to the latest added block.

It's okay if you don't understand what you have just read. You'll learn more about this complex network as we go along.

Blockchain in Detail

The blockchain is regarded as the primary technological innovation of Bitcoin, because it serves as proof of all the exchanges on the network. A block is the latest part of a blockchain that records a portion or the entire current transactions, which when completed will be permanently recorded in the database. Every time a block is completed, a new block will be created.

There are numerous blocks in the blockchain, so some are asking if they are randomly added in the blockchain. These blocks are not randomly added as they are connected to each other similar to a chain in a chronological and linear order, with each block containing a hash of the past block.

To better explain the concept of blockchain, let's use the analogy with traditional banking. Blockchain is similar to the entire history of transactions that happened in the bank. Bitcoin transactions are added chronologically in a blockchain similar to bank transactions. On the other hand, blocks can be regarded as separate bank statements.

According to the protocol followed by Bitcoin, the blockchain database will be shared by all nodes that participate in the system. The entire copy of the blockchain has records of each Bitcoin transaction. Therefore, it can provide insights about important details, such as the value of a certain address at any period in the past.

At present, most of us put our trust to the middlemen in our financial transactions, such as banks. The blockchain system gets rid of the middlemen as suppliers and customers can connect directly, which makes the third party (banks) unnecessary.

Through secured cryptography to keep the transactions safe, blockchain offers a decentralized database or digital ledger of transactions, which everyone in the network could see. This network is basically a chain of computers that should unanimously approve the transaction before it could be confirmed and recorded.

Why is Blockchain Revolutionary?

Blockchain is revolutionary because it could work for any type of transaction as long as it involves anything valuable such as money, property, or goods. Its possible uses are endless: from purchasing items online, sending money overseas, paying for services, or collecting taxes. It can also eliminate fraud as each transaction will be recorded and accessible on a public ledger, which can be seen by anyone.

Who Is Using Blockchain?

For now, only a few people use blockchain, mostly those working online. But theoretically, if it becomes widespread and common, anyone who has access to the internet could use blockchain for any type of transaction.

Based on a survey conducted by the Global Agenda Council of the World Economic Forum, only a very slim percentage of worldwide GDP (about $20 billion or 0.025%) is stored in the blockchain at the present. However, experts project that this will dramatically increase in the next few years as financial institutions and technological firms consider the system as a way to increase the pace of transactions and minimize costs.

Global companies are now starting to use blockchain, including IBM, Microsoft, and UBS. Even national banks (such as Bank of Canada) are now experimenting with this technology. According to a report released by Aite, a financial technology consulting firm, about $75 million have been spent on blockchain by banks around the world. On top of that, the number of venture capitalists (mostly from Silicon Valley) is growing.

Blockchain Can Be Significant and Disruptive Across Many Industries

Companies often secure their digital data by building a wall surrounding it. Sadly, this could expose it to people who could find a way to access the data and penetrate inside the walls, which include unscrupulous administrators with full authority to access to digital information.

Meanwhile, transactions and information systems in the blockchain framework don't allow changes to data once it is recorded, unless all or part of the participating nodes verify the change. This is a primary shift from the conventional "wall" because it minimizes the opportunity for concealed transactions. This feature makes blockchain significant for organizations in any industry that want to secure their data.

In a conventional process, a system administrator with bad motives could possibly make changes in the historical transactions, because he or she has access to data. But with a blockchain system across data servers, you need a whole team of nodes working together to change the data. This significantly decreases the possibility of data manipulation. It is very difficult to modify any data if the framework is widespread. Blockchain technology is well-distributed across several data servers, making it difficult to launch attack on both software and hardware.

The financial sector is the leading industry that explores the uses of blockchain mainly for transactions involving cryptocurrencies. Bitcoin utilizes blockchain technology. Currently, there are 11 banks that formed the R3 consortium to connect on the Ethereum blockchain network. In 2013, the Estonian government already used blockchain-based technology to verify data in their servers.

However, blockchain also has the ability to increase security between data exchanges, because it makes data transfer easy between parties.

Blockchain in the Healthcare Industry

By utilizing electronic signatures on blockchain-based information, which provides access only when verified by several nodes, healthcare institutions could control the accessibility and maintenance of private health records. Moreover, groups of healthcare stakeholders such as doctors, clinics, patients, and insurance companies could be integrated in the overall blockchain, which will reduce fraud in healthcare transactions.

Blockchain in the Legal Sector

Through blockchains, it is possible to contain a large amount of data, which includes contracts and digital copies of records, paper trails, and other information that can aid in legal proceedings. The effect of "smart contracts", which refers to protocols that enforce or facilitate contract performance through the use of blockchain – will have significant effect on industries. Smart contracts eliminate the use of third parties like law firms, because payments could be processed based on specific milestones. Through the smart contracts protocol, agreements can be easily monitored electronically, generating a powerful escrow by taking out the control from only one entity.

Blockchain in the Defense Field

Unsanctioned changes or access of important defense infrastructure (like network firmware and operating systems) can severely compromise national security. For most states, defense framework and computer systems are distributed across various locations. Blockchain technology distributed across several data centers could boost security against attacks on critical networks and hardware by ensuring layers access for changes.

Blockchain in the Energy Industry

Generating electricity at the micro level is now becoming a popular trend among power generators. New initiatives in the energy sector (such as home power generation and community solar power) are filling in gaps of power supply across the globe. As this trend adds to conventional suppliers of energy, it fosters the creation of an energy market. Smart meters could register the production and consumption of electricity in a blockchain. This will allow for consumption of the surplus in another location, which provides currency or credits to the original generator. The currency could then be redeemed against the power grid when the microgeneration requires more energy. Through blockchain, these contracts could be enforced in real time, allowing the energy market to be facilitated with less bureaucracy.

Blockchain in Government Service

Government organizations that are working in silos may cause the process of information exchange to be slow, which has negative effects on the delivery of service. Through blockchain, the data could be exchanged between departments because the framework could ensure that the data will be released in real time, even when government departments and the public have agreed to share access to the data. Blockchain technology can improve transparency as well as keep the proper checks and balances.

With such wide-range use for block chain technology, there's no surprise that it has the potential to improve the quality of service delivery while improving integrity and confidentiality of data. With its advantage of providing security and transparency in transactions, blockchain is positioned to change how we live.

But before that, let's explore how blockchain works. Proceed to the next Chapter.

Chapter 2 - How Blockchain Works

The blockchain technology is regarded as one of the best inventions of the Information Age. It is innovative and disruptive, because it allows exchange of values without the need to go through a centralized channel.

Let's say that two friends, Peter and John, made a $100 bet on the weather in New York tomorrow. Peter bets it will be rainy, while Jon bets it will be sunny. There are three options to take care of this bet:

1. The winning one will get the $100 at stake. This will be easy because Peter and John can trust each other, as they are friends. But, there is always the risk of not fulfilling the promise.

2. Peter and John can enter into a binding contract. Through a written contract, they will be more compelled to pay. And if Peter fails to pay John, he has to pay the added money for the legal cost and the decision may even take months or even years. And for just $100, this is not practical.

3. Peter and John can get the services of a third party. Each will provide $50 to the third party, and will award the amount to the winner. But there is also the risk that the third party will run with the money. So, Peter and John may end up with the first two options: trust or contract.

However, both trust and contract are not even the best solutions. Would you trust a stranger? Are you willing to spend time and money to enforce a contract? Blockchain technology is revolutionary because it provides a third option that is fast, affordable, and safe.

Through blockchain, Peter and John can write a short line of code on the blockchain framework that will both send $50. The framework will keep the $100 secured and based on the weather in New York tomorrow, will automatically send the total amount to the winner. They can verify the logic of the contract, and when it is already running on the blockchain, it will be impossible to modify or cancel. This effort could seem too high level for a simple bet, but let's say you have to sell a car or a whole company?

The goal of this Chapter is to discuss how the blockchain technology works without providing you with jargon. We'll just cover the basic details just to provide you an overview of the mechanisms and logic behind blockchain.

Bitcoin is regarded as the most popular application of blockchain. Bitcoin is a digital currency that anyone can use to facilitate the exchange of goods as well as services. This is similar to the Euro, Dollars, RMB, and currencies issued and controlled by government banks around the world. We will describe Bitcoin to demonstrate how blockchain technology works.

Bitcoin 101

One unit of the digital Bitcoin currency is One Bitcoin. Just like the logic behind the dollar, which has no actual value, BTC has also no natural value, but it becomes valuable because a group of people come into agreement to exchange goods as well as services. In order to monitor the value of BTC that a person has, the framework uses a blockchain ledger, which is an electronic file that monitors all transactions involving a Bitcoin.

LEDGER	
Owner	Value
Peter	234
John	56
Andrew	7
Zachary	32
Julius	89
Sarah	1236
Mary	32
Elton	11

Fig. 1 - Simple Ledger

The ledger is not controlled by a centralized server such as a banking firm or by a single data server. This is disseminated across several data centers through a series of privately-owned computers, which perform data storage and computations. Every computer signifies a node in the network and stores a replicated file of the ledger.

For example, let's say Sarah would like to pay BTC to Elton, he sends a broadcast to the whole network saying that the value of BTCs in her account will be decreased by 10 BTC and the value of his account will be increased by the same value. Every node connected to the blockchain network will be sent with this message and will confirm the transaction request to their file ledger, which will all update the balances of Sara and Elton's blockchain wallet.

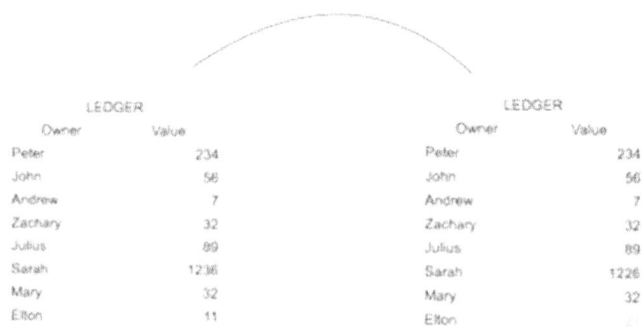

Fig. 2 Simplified message for requesting transaction in blockchain

Instead of a single centralized unit such as a bank or a finance firm, a network of computers perform the ledger's maintenance.

This framework has several effects:

- In the banking system, individuals are only aware of their own account balances and transactions; on the decentralized network, anyone can see the transactions of the whole network.

- Although you can trust the banking system in general, the network of Bitcoin is disseminated and if there's something wrong with the system, you can't call a customer service hotline or hold someone responsible.

- The blockchain network is created in such manner that trust is not required, as reliability and security are obtained through special mathematical codes and functions.

To facilitate any transaction within the decentralized network, you have to gain access to a wallet, which is a system of code allowing you to store and trade your BTCs. Because theoretically, only you can spend your BTCs, every wallet is encrypted by a unique cryptography system, which utilizes a special combination of different yet linked keys: a public key and a private key.

The public key will secure the message, which can only be accessed by the owner using his or her private key. On the other hand, only a linked public key can be used to decrypt a message that has been secured by a private key.

To send BTCs, Sarah has to send the message that is secured using the private key of her wallet, so she could only spend the BTCs she holds as Elton has the unique access to his private key required for wallet access. Every node connected in the blockchain framework could verify that the request for transaction originates from Sarah through the decryption of the message using Elton's public key.

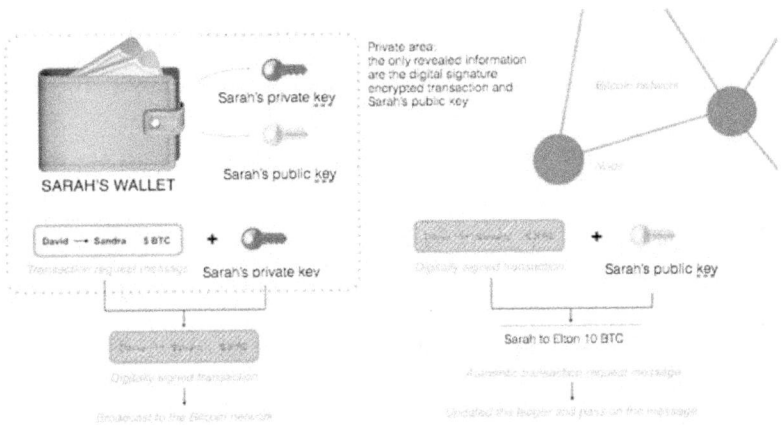

Fig. 3 System-generated signature in the blockchain network

In encrypting the request for transaction with the private key of the wallet, the system will digitally generate a signature, which is utilized by the decentralized framework to verify the origin and check if the transaction is authentic. The generated signature is composed of text strings, which are combinations of the transaction request plus the private key of the sender. Hence, it will not be recognized for other transaction requests. Once you change a single entry in the request message for transaction, the signature will be modified by the system. No possible attacker can modify the transaction requests or change the value of BTCs that you want to send.

The public keys in the wallet are sent to the nodes within the BTC framework. So, if you are sending BTCs to another person, you're really delivering value to their wallet's public key. In order to send BTCs, you have to verify that you have the wallet's private key, because this is required to secure the message for transaction request. Take note that because you are broadcasting the request after the encryption process, there's no need to disclose your wallet's private key.

Every node connected to the blockchain will keep a copy of the ledger. As shown in Fig. 1, the blockchain framework does not monitor the balances of the account, because it is only recording each requested transaction. In fact, the ledger does not monitor balances. It only monitors each transaction inside the Bitcoin system as shown in Fig. 4. In order to know the balance in the wallet, you have to evaluate and confirm all transactions (that happened on the entire framework) linked to your account.

LEDGER

Transactions	Value
Peter to Zoe	23
John to Julie	0.89
Sarah to Elton	10
Zachary to Rob	1.56
Ryan to Bob	9.2
Stacy to Gwen	3.24
Mary to Phoebe	2.5
Elton to Zoe	4.8

Fig. 4 A basic format of ledger used in a blockchain

Balance verification is done through connections to past transactions. To send BTCs to Gwen, Stacy has to create a request for transaction, which involves connections to the past transactions (incoming) with balance equal or exceeding 3.24 BTCs. These links are regarded as inputs, and the nodes within system shall confirm that the entire value of the transactions will equal or exceed 3.24 BTCs, as well as verify that these incoming transactions are not yet complete or that the BTCs have not yet been spent. As a matter of fact, whenever someone refers inputs for a transaction, these are regarded as invalid for future transactions. And so, this will be automatically performed in Stacy's wallet and cross checked by the nodes within the BTC network. She will only send 3.24 BTCs to Gwen's wallet through her public key.

In order for the system to verify the transaction inputs and recognize them as valid, it has to check all the past transactions, which are interlinked to the account being used to transmit BTCs through the confirmations, which every node received as transaction inputs. In order to make this simple and hasten the authentication process, a unique ledger of transactions that are not yet complete is recorded within the nodes connected to the network. Through this verification layer, it is impossible to initiate double spending for your received BTCs.

The program that facilitates exchanges on the BTC framework is open source. Hence, any person who can use a computer that is connected to the internet can facilitate transactions. But, if there are errors within the code utilized to disseminate messages to request transactions, the relevant BTC will be lost forever. Remember, because the blockchain framework is public, there's no technical support – there's no one to help you resolve problems related to any transaction or help you remember your forgotten password or key.

Is Blockchain Safe?

Anyone who knows how to use a computer can use and facilitate exchanges in the BTC network through a concealed link such as VPN or TOR, and send or receive cryptocurrencies by providing only his or her public key.

Moreover, the number of BTC addresses that can be generated is 1461501437330912918205684839716283719655932542976 or 2^{160}. The large number safeguards the blockchain from threats without restricting anyone to have their own Bitcoin wallet.

However, blockchain is not a risk-free system. Messages for transaction requests are sent from every node inside the network. Thus, the order for two transactions connected for every node could be different. One way to launch an attack is to send BTCs, stand by for the other party to deliver the product, then submit a request to reverse the transaction to the original wallet. In such situation, there are nodes that have already received the new request before the original request. The original transaction will be deemed invalid because the request enters results that are already confirmed as spent.

If this occurs, the nodes connected to the network could disagree with each other about the transaction sequence they have received. The BTC network initiates exchanges by placing them in a single block, wherein every block contains a fixed value of transactions and a connection to the original block. Hence, blocks are organized into chronological and linear order, which provides the nomenclature for the entire network – blockchain.

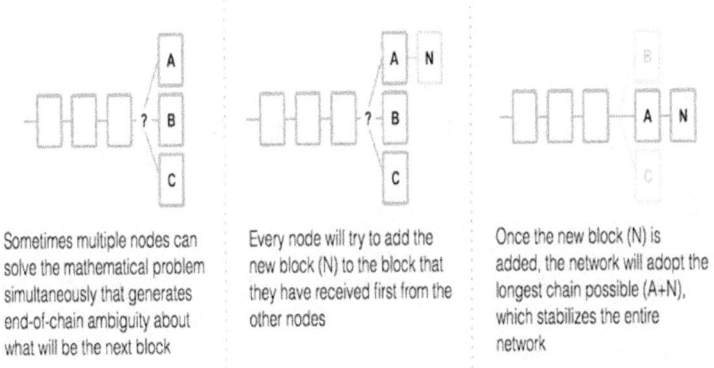

Fig. 5 End of Chain Ambiguity Logic

The conflict about what block will represent the chain's end will open up the possibility for fraud – such as when an exchange occurs within a block connected to the shorter tail (see B-block in Figure 5). After solving the succeeding block, the transaction could be reinstated to the unconfirmed transaction similar to all other requests in the B-Block.

Look at how Alfred can take advantage of this flaw to facilitate double spending. Alfred transmits money to

Robert, Robert then delivers the goods to Alfred. Because nodes often recognize the tail that's longer than that of the verified transaction, if Alfred can create a longer tail containing a reverse transaction with similar references as input, Robert will lose both his product and BTC.

How does the framework prevent this type of fraud? Every block contains a confirmation for the past block, and this reference is linked to the mathematical problem, which should be solved to broadcast the block to the system. Hence, it is extremely difficult to pre-calculate a line of blocks because you need to guess the answer to solve the block and connect it to the blockchain.

Alfred is in a race against the remaining network to solve the mathematical problem, which will allow him to include the next block to the chain. And even if he solves it before anyone else, it's unlikely that he can solve two, three, or more blocks in a series, because he has to compete against thousands of nodes connected to the framework.

There is the possibility that Alfred can use a super fast PC to create sufficient sequential guesses to go against the entire network to solve blocks. But this is still impossible because of the sheer number of computers linked to the system. Alfred cannot provide the answers to numerous blocks at the precise time required to complete double spending.

Meanwhile, transactions are getting more secure with time. Those integrated in blocks that have been verified in the past are safer than the ones included in the last block. Because a block is integrated to the chain every 10 minutes on average, waiting for about an hour for when the transaction is added in a block for the first time provides a higher chance that the transaction will be processed and becomes irreversible.

To facilitate the sending of BTCs, you have to reference a transaction, which sends Bitcoin to your wallet – and this could apply to all the transactions which will take place in the network. To balance the deflationary nature of BTC due to software errors and lost passwords, a reward could be provided to those that will solve the mathematical problem of every block. The activity of running the BTC blockchain software to obtain these BTC rewards is known as mining.

This reward is the primary incentive, which drives private individuals to operate the nodes. Hence, it provides the required computing power required to process BTC transactions and to stabilize the blockchain system.

Because it will take a long time for a regular computer to solve a block (average of one year), nodes could be integrated in groups, dividing the number of guesses that each node has to try to solve the next block. As such, it is faster for the group to guess the right number and obtain the reward, which will be shared among the group members. These groups are known as mining pools.

These mining pools are quite large and signify more than 20% of the entire network computing power. This has obvious implications for network security as demonstrated in the double-spending attack. Even if these pools can possibly obtain half the network's computing power, the way to the chain can be difficult to control. But some of these mining pools that have gained significant computing power restrict the number of their members to protect the entire network's security.

Since the whole network's computing power is likely to increase over time given the technological innovation and the increasing number of nodes, the blockchain system will recalibrate the problem difficulty to find the answer to the next block, targeting 10 minutes on average for the entire network. This will ensure overall security as well as network stability.

Furthermore, every four years, the block reward will be reduced by half, so mining bitcoin could become less exciting in time. To avoid the nodes from stopping in running the network, small reward fees could be linked to every transaction. These rewards will be collected by the node, which successfully involve such transactions in a block and solves the mathematical problem.

Because of this framework, the transactions associated with higher rewards are often processed faster compared to those linked with a low reward. So, when you are sending a transaction, you have the option whether to process it faster or slower. The transaction fees in the BTC network are presently minimal if compared with what the banks are charging and are not linked with the value of the transaction.

Last **Bitcoin** blocks

Block height	Block created	Transactions	Block fee	Size (kb)	Days destroyed
441865	5 minutes ago	2648	0.85594077	975.79 kB	94,035.35
441864	23 minutes ago	2448	0.87642498	974.65 kB	9,900.30
441863	47 minutes ago	2456	0.93449546	974.75 kB	6,917.26
441862	1 hour 18 minutes ago	2406	0.75373267	975.80 kB	6,129.73
441861	1 hour 30 minutes ago	483	0.14720262	974.77 kB	4,257.95
441860	1 hour 32 minutes ago	2263	0.60341872	974.63 kB	8,990.04
441859	1 hour 36 minutes ago	2692	0.86478309	974.79 kB	8,069.90
441858	2 hours 1 minute ago	1144	0.28381792	425.66 kB	7,118.84
441857	2 hours 3 minutes ago	2742	0.80513080	974.75 kB	4,083.56
441856	2 hours 23 minutes ago	890	0.20156068	306.12 kB	6,746.77
441855	2 hours 26 minutes ago	751	0.21079350	265.26 kB	2,581.31

Fig. 6 Bitcoin Transactions

Now that you have a basic understanding of how the blockchain technology works, it's time to have a fast look at why it is revolutionary. Blockchain has several significant advantages:

- You have total control of the value you own. No third party has control of the value or that could limit your access.

- The fee to facilitate a value transaction is very minimal. This is exciting for those who need to process small payments.

- Money can be sent in a few minutes and the transaction could be considered safe in a few hours, and not days like in a bank transaction.

- Because anyone can check each transaction on the block chain, there is full transparency.

- You can take advantage of the blockchain technology to create decentralized applications, which will make it easy to manage data and transfer value safely and fast.

But there are several challenges that should be addressed:

- Similar to other cryptocurrencies, BTC is highly volatile. Take note that Bitcoins are still considered rare if you compare it with national currencies, and so the demand changes from time to time. The price of BTC is highly affected by significant events or news in the cryptocurrency world.

- You can send and receive anonymous transactions. While this protects privacy, there is also the risk of illegal activities facilitated over the network.

- Blockchain technology is still in its infancy. Innovative tools are being developed each day to improve stability, while at the same time providing a wide range of features, services, and tools.

- Even if most exchange platforms are rising, it is still not that easy to exchange BTC for services and goods. But these are becoming very popular.

In general, the blockchain technology is projected to revolutionize different industries from energy distribution to advertising. Its primary advantage lies in its ability to eliminate the need to rely on a centralized organization.

Chapter 3 - Blockchains and Internet of Things

Blockchain is starting to play a crucial role in the Internet of Things (IoT) by improving security, allowing low-cost devices to be scalable, and making it easier to manage devices.

But before discussing the role of blockchains in IoT, let's briefly discuss IoT and discover why it is significant in our modern world.

What is Internet of Things (IoT)?

Many have already encountered the phrase "Internet of Things" or IoT, but ignored to understand this technology assuming that it is just another fancy tech or app that you can find on the Internet. But

IoT is far beyond a fad, because it has the potential to affect how we live as well as how we work.

So, what precisely is IoT and what will be its effect on how we live? Despite of the simplicity of its name, IoT is in fact layered in complexities. In this chapter, we will try to cover the basics. Let's start by understanding some fundamental concepts about IoT.

Broadband Internet is becoming very popular. Hence, it is becoming cheaper to connect to the internet. Meanwhile, more and more gadgets and devices are being created with Wi-Fi capabilities and built-in sensors. Smartphones are very common nowadays, and producing technology to support these innovations is now affordable. These things are favorable for IoT.

Basically, IoT is the concept of connecting anything that is electronic (or even not) to the Internet. This includes everything around you when you are at work (computer, cellphone, wireless speaker, headphones, coffee makers, water dispenser) or when you are at home (lamp, washing machine, clock, TV) and almost everything there is. IoT is also applicable to machine parts such as the drill of an oil rig or the jet engine of an airbus.

According to the projection of the analyst firm Gartner, more than 26 billion devices will be connected to the Internet by the year 2020. This a significant volume of devices that could interact online. Some experts even project higher numbers reaching to at least 100 billion.

You can consider IoT as a vast network of things connected online, and this includes people. The connection will be people to things, people to people, and things to things.

What is the Effect of IoT on Your Life?

In the future, we will live by the rule that anything that can connect will be connected. But is there really such a need for things to be connected online? There are many futuristic concepts, ideas, and videos showing what the future will look like or what possible value it could provide for us.

For example, in the future, you are driving to work to attend a meeting – your car will be capable of accessing your calendar and will plan the fastest route. If the traffic is heavy, your car can even access your phone to send a message to your colleagues that you will be late for how many minutes. Your alarm clock will not only ring at 5 a.m. but it is also connected to your coffee maker and will send an instruction to start brewing. At the office, your photocopier keeps track of the paper supply and will place an order whenever necessary.

On a larger scale, the IoT could be used in transportation systems and waste management. There are now smart cities that are using IoT to improve efficiency and reduce waste. This innovation could help us understand and enhance how we live, work, and relax.

This vision is now starting to take place. It is actually not difficult to see how and why IoT is creating a buzz today, because it will surely open a lot of opportunities (as well as challenges) ahead. One issue that is often brought up against IoT is security.

With billions of things connected to the Internet, it could be hard to believe that the information collected by these things will be safe. What if someone hacks into your coffee maker and becomes capable of tapping into your whole network to siphon vital information such as your bank details, credit card numbers, or personal routine?

There are also concerns about data sharing and privacy. These concerns are now being debated by those who are for and against IoT, so we can only imagine how the topic will escalate if we are talking about billions of devices linked with each other and are able to communicate with one another.

Some of these concerns can be addressed by using blockchain technology.

Blockchain Creates Trust with Transparency and Accountability

Blockchain can help in establishing trust, transparency, and accountability when it comes to streamlining the process for IoT.

The existing ecosystem of IoT depend on centralized communication framework that is based on a server-client system. The devices are recognized, verified, and linked using cloud servers that are able to process and store large data capacities. The connection between the devices will have to go through online, even if they are just inches away from each other.

Although this framework has linked basic computing devices for many years, and will surely continue to support low-scale IoT networks today, it won't be able to respond to the future needs of the growing IoT framework.

Current IoT solutions carry high costs, because of the infrastructure and maintenance cost associated with centralized servers, costly networking equipment, and big server farms. The mere volume of communications, which will have to be managed when IoT gadgets expand to the billions of devices, will substantially increase the costs.

Even if the engineering challenges are resolved, the acquisition and maintenance of cloud servers will still become a roadblock and a weak point, which could disrupt the whole network.

Meanwhile, the ownership between devices is so diverse and the need for cloud infrastructure makes the communication between machines very difficult. There's no unified platform, which integrates all devices and there's no assurance that cloud services provided by various manufacturers are compatible and interoperable.

Decentralized Networks for IoT

A decentralized approach to networking IoT will resolve most of the current concerns in IoT. Using a standardized communication framework to process the vast value of transactions between devices will considerably decrease the costs related with installing and maintaining huge centralized data centers, and could disseminate the need for computation and storage across the billions of devices that form the IoT system. This can stop any risk of failure in the nodes connected to the network from bringing the whole system to the brink of collapse.

But establishing communication between peers can present its own challenges, primarily about security. And of course, security in IoT is far beyond safeguarding critical data. The possible solution is to keep privacy and security in large IoT networks and provide some method for validation and consensus for transactions to thwart theft and spoofing.

To facilitate the functions of conventional IoT solutions away from centralized control, any decentralized approach should provide the following basic functions:

1. Disseminated file sharing

2. P2p broadcast

3. Independent device connection

The Blockchain Solution

One advantage of using blockchain for IoT is that the process will be public. Everyone who participates could see the blocks as well as the surrounding transaction. As we have discussed in the previous chapters, this doesn't mean that all could see the actual transaction details, because these are protected by the owner's private key.

Remember, blockchain is decentralized. Hence, there's no single authority that should approve the transaction or stipulate certain rules to accept the transaction. So, there's a large amount of trust involved, because all the participants in the network should reach a consensus to recognize and verify the transactions. The transactions are also secure. The database could only be extended and past records cannot be modified.

Blockchain technology can help IoT attain scalability, reliability, and privacy. Some experts regard blockchain as the silver bullet that could help IoT to reach its peak. It could be used to track the billions of devices connected to the Internet, facilitate the communication between devices, and enable the processing of transactions.

The decentralized approach to IoT can eliminate single points of failure, which creates a more flexible ecosystem for devices. The secured algorithms utilized by blockchains can increase the privacy of consumer data.

It is impossible to tamper or manipulate with the ledger, because it does not exist in one location. Likewise, middle-men attacks cannot be launched because there's no single link of communication that could be intercepted. Blockchain allows transparent and secure P2P messaging, which has already proven its value in the financial world through the Bitcoin, which provides safe P2P payment services without the need for external brokers.

The decentralized nature of blockchain makes it a good composition to become a basic element of IoT solutions. It is not surprising that some IoT technologies have easily become among the early users of blockchain.

By using blockchain as a fundamental technology in IoT, the system can allow secure transaction between devices. In this framework, the blockchain could consider message exchanges between devices similar to Bitcoin transactions. To allow messages to pass through, the devices can take advantage of smart contracts that will handle the agreement between the parties involved.

In this framework, it is easy to connect sensors even if they are miles away, allowing for direct communication between important components (such as the mechanism of irrigation systems to regulate water flow based on the detected factors on the crops). Utilizing blockchain technology could enable genuine autonomous devices, which could transmit data or even facilitate complex processes without passing through a centralized broker. This kind of autonomy is doable because the nodes within the blockchain network can verify the validity of the transaction without depending on a centralized function.

Chapter 4 - Blockchains and Cryptocurrencies

In the ancient world, the commodities that are crucial for daily living were regarded as money (chickens and cows) and bartered within the community or across trading partners. Then, the rise of modern society and urban centers brought the need to monitor money as well as value through wide territories. This has resulted in the emergence of money in paper and coin form issued by the government.

With the emergence of the Internet, it is very easy nowadays to buy and sell anything regardless of the time and location with the help of credit cards issued by banks. Credit cards became a wide substitute for traditional money and facilitated payments in electronic form.

And then recently, a new form of money, which harnesses the power of the internet was born - cryptocurrency. In this chapter, we will explore what cryptocurrencies are, find out how they work, and reveal the significance of blockchain to their usage.

What are Cryptocurrencies?

Cryptocurrencies (also known as cryptomoney or cryptoassets) are a medium of trade similar to government-issued currencies, albeit utilizing cryptography to make the exchange of digital information safe and transparent. Cryptocurrency is seen as the next stage in the evolution of money. Most of the things in our world has become digital, so will be our way of buying and selling goods as well as services.

Cryptocurrencies offer a sustainable approach of monitoring the ownership of unique electronic representations of value, which we call money. These are fully self-contained systems, which both regulate and monitor every unit of cryptocurrency. Every unit serves like a piece of information that works around a network. The units of cryptocurrency could be as small as $0.01 or as big as $1 Billion. Some cryptocurrencies are centralized (controlled by one organization) while others are decentralized (controlled by the public).

Cryptocurrencies use different time stamping methods, so that there's no need for a trusted external party to confirm the transactions integrated to the blockchain ledger as we have already discussed in the previous chapters. For example, in Bitcoin, the system uses a proof-of-work approach that is known as Mining. Other forms of cryptocurrencies achieve the same result with alternative systems, which are usually regarded as Consensus Platforms or Consensus Protocols.

Forms of Cryptocurrencies

Bitcoin, which we have discussed in Chapter 2, is a form of cryptocurrency, and regarded as the most popular among available forms of cryptocurrencies today. This is due to the fact that Bitcoin is the first cryptocurrency that has successfully proven the viability of a digital exchange of money that is secured by cryptography and is accessible for everyone.

But similar to different currencies around the world, there are also other forms of cryptocurrencies. In fact, there are about 1,000 various types of cryptocurrencies that are currently traded on the coin market cap, which is the popular domain for searching and monitoring the prices of cryptocurrencies.

Below are the top forms of cryptocurrencies that you can use as an alternative to Bitcoin.

Litecoin

Litecoin was introduced in 2011. LTC is regarded as the silver Bitcoin, because it is also based on the protocol used by BTC. However, this is designed to ensure that mining will be more affordable and more transparent compared to BTC.

Peercoin

Peercoin was introduced in 2012. PPC is also based on the Bitcoin protocol, but it utilizes a different approach to confirm mined coins. Rather than depending on the proof-of-work (POW) system that requires miners to resolve hashes, PPC will eventually implement a POS or proof-of-stake approach. In the POS approach, the higher the coins you accumulate, the higher your chances to mine more coins. PPC doesn't have a fixed upper limit of coins, and so it is considered as a currency that is vulnerable to inflation.

Namecoin

Namecoin was introduced in 2011. NMC was not intended to be used as a currency. Rather, its primary purpose is to regulate an alternative DNS or Domain Name System for the .bit domain, which can escape censorship because it exists outside the control of the Internet Corporation for Assigned Names and Numbers (ICANN).

Novacoin

Novacoin was introduced in 2013. NVC is a fork of PPC, and thus shares similarities with PPC hybrid POW/POS systems. But NVC takes a leaf out of LTC book and uses script hashing for the POW approach. NVC is also more difficult when it comes to POS as compared to PPC. Moreover, NVC has a maximum total supply of 2 B NVC, even though it is believed that it is unlikely to achieve this limit.

Primecoin

Primecoin was introduced in 2013. The primary difference of XPM from most cryptocurrencies is that mining doesn't involve resolving hashes. Rather, XPM mining involves searching for Cunningham chains (specific prime number sequences). These prime numbers are said to be more mathematically valuable compared to hashes, which are often decoded in cryptocurrency mining and are used in everything from cryptography of public key and number theory.

Quarkcoin

Qurakcoin was introduced in 2013. QRK is considered as the best cryptocurrency for those concerned with security. It implements nine sequences of hashing, which chooses from six various methods of hashing. Other cryptocurrencies use a single hash, and so QRK has a natural security edge over them. QRK utilizes CPU mining, and similar to PPC, doesn't have solid cap on its total number.

Zetacoin

Zetacoin was introduced in 2013. ZET is also derived from BTC. However, it stakes its claim in two distinct approaches. Mainly, it has a faster block rate compared to BTC. Hence, the speed of completing the transaction is 20x faster than BTC. Take note that ZET is an inflationary cryptocurrency.

Feathercoin

Feathercoin was introduced in 2013. FTC is also a direct derivative of LTC, and it is very similar to LTC. However, it still has several distinctions that make it unique. FTC adjusts its difficulty of mining more frequently compared to LTC. In addition, FTC is also implementing Advanced Checkpointing, which is a security measure intended to safeguard against most attacks used to thwart transactions.

Digitalcoin

Digitalcoin was introduced in 2013. DGC is derived from LTC, which is intended to keep its value and boosts its stability. It easily retargets the mining ecosystem and optimizes performance. Also, the DGC block rewards decrease at a slower rate compared to other cryptocurrencies.

Stablecoin

Stablecoin was introduced in 2013. An interesting feature of SBC is that it comes with a built-in coin integration service. This makes certain that SBC transactions are untraceable and encrypted. Moreover, SBC is active in promoting its currency worldwide and has even launched a website in Chinese to market SBC in China and rest of Asia.

Significance of Blockchain in Trading Cryptocurrencies

The cryptocurrencies described above are all using blockchains to provide secure and transparent exchange. Because cryptocurrency is electronic and cannot be counterfeited, it is considered more viable than credit cards (which can be arbitrarily reversed by the sender through a chargeback).

Blockchain also makes it unnecessary for a third party to handle exchange of cryptocurrency and safeguards wealth against capital controls. Because cryptocurrencies are essentially electronic, the location of the traders becomes irrelevant as you can initiate and complete transactions anytime and anywhere.

Through blockchain, the transaction for cryptocurrencies can be highly anonymous or non-disclosure. This is highly attractive to traders who want to be private in their dealings. It also encourages free exchange of regulatory parties and promotes affordable banking, because it's possible to complete a transaction anytime and anywhere as long as the traders have access to the internet.

Cryptocurrency also utilizes push methodology, which allows the holder of cryptocurrency to send precisely what is required by the recipient with no other details required. This can help in preventing identity theft as seen with credit card use, where you have to entrust your credit card details to the vendor, making you vulnerable to fraudulent activities.

In general, financial services can be cheaper as there are usually no transaction fees for trading cryptocurrencies as miners are rewarded by the network.

Finally, with blockchain and cryptocurrency, the trader is in full ownership of the account, which is not similar to other digital currency systems where there is a need for a third-party to manage the account. Through blockchain, you have to own the private key as well as the corresponding public key that makes up for the address.

Chapter 5 - Ethereum Investment Opportunities

If you have noticed in the previous chapter, most forms of cryptocurrencies were introduced in 2013, which is considered as the 'gold rush' for digital money. That year, the price of cryptocurrencies increased from $126 to more than $1,100 from October to November 2013.

Hence, cryptocurrencies became an attractive investment for investors who want adventure. Because of the relative age of cryptocurrencies, these are still under significant volatility if you compare them to traditional currencies and assets such as bonds or stocks.

But for investors, volatility creates opportunities for making profit and with the maturity of cryptocurrency traders, investors are analyzing other forms of cryptocurrencies (aside from BTC) to possibly generate profitable investment returns.

One form of cryptocurrency is the ether from Ethereum that has obtained the second largest market capitalization for all cryptocurrencies in just a short span of time.

Introduction to Ethereum

Ethereum refers to a decentralized ecosystem which manages smart contracts – applications that perform without the possibility of censorship, downtime, fraud, or external interference.

Ethereum has been designed for developers to generate their own applications, which could represent movement of value or ownership from one entity to another. Moreover, it facilitates an if-then form of smart contracts that will be integrated into the blockchain to generate binding terms for contracts.

There is wide use for the Ethereum technology, and it also has the power to be disruptive of the traditional platform for vast types of industries. Anyone can make smart contracts on the blockchain used by Ethereum to signify ownership of intellectual property, financial securities, deeds, and any type of contract in a safe and decentralized platform.

Introduction to Ether (ETH)

The Ethereum network uses Ether (ETH) as its cryptocurrency. It is different to BTC and other cryptocurrencies, because it is not designed to be used for financial transactions but instead it is intended to become the fuel that powers the Etherium blockchain.

Hence, those who use their computers to confirm transactions or contribute to the progress of the blockchain used by Ethereum will be provided with Ether. So to some extent, it follows a similar approach to BTC mining. If you need to perform particular operations on the Ethereum blockchain, you have to pay Ether.

Ether is also different from BTC in the way it is designed. The Ether supply is determined as such: the 1st batch of Ether was generated as a component of a crowdfunding initiative in 2014. This initial offer has generated 60 Million Ethers for the collaborators of the pre-sale. About 12 Million Ether has been allocated to the development fund of Ethereum that involves early developers and contributors. Moreover, 5 ETH has been generated for each block mined based on the website of Ethereum. Thus, the original

ETH supply was 72 million. But there's no fixed figure for ETH. In fact, about 18 million ETH are generated each year.

The supply limits are subject to change as the system is now working on a new algorithm known as Casper. This update is expected to require less power for mining. Hence, there is a possibility for increasing supply. This will also play a crucial role in the future price levels of ETH.

Important exchanges like the GDAX CoinBase now supports Ether, enabling investors to buy ETH with BTC or any flat currency. This facilitates easy access for new investors who are interested in trading on the ETH market. Moreover, a new organization known as EtherIndex has already been registered with the US Securities and Exchange Commission (SEC) to launch ETF fund.

The ETF fund will allow investors to invest indirectly in this underlying asset similar to stocks or bonds, real estate, commodities, as well as other forms of cryptocurrencies. This is attractive for those having second thoughts about investing in cryptocurrencies because of several concerns (including storage safety). Once the ETF fund for Ether becomes viable for investments, ETH will experience a substantial boost because the issuer of ETF has to buy Ether each time someone purchases ETF shares.

Ether's Price Development

Because of the anonymous nature of cryptocurrency wallets, it can be difficult to say where the demand for a specific cryptocurrency will come from, and it is even more difficult to project where the cryptocurrency price will move. Some speculators have decided to trade cryptocurrency to make quick returns. Developments in cryptocurrency prices include Ether, which is often linked with public interest and media coverage that could be monitored through online tools such as Google Trends.

Since August 2015 when Ether became tradable, the price of ETH has been significantly volatile. It experienced a steep rally in the First Quarter of 2016, moving from $1 to surpassing $10 for every Ether in March. Ether hit its latest peak in April at $21.50 when the DOA was attacked and almost $50 million worth of Ether was lost.

This resulted to a crash, which almost slashed the ETH price. After only a few hours, the Ether price has oscillated in the $10 to $15 range. The overall value of ETC and ETH has seen stability going forward, while the theoretically opposed parts are independently still highly volatile in the hard-fork fallout.

The Viability of Investing in Ether

Ether managed to become the second largest cryptocurrency within a very short span of time. This is proof of the viability of Ethereum as a significant blockchain technology today and in the future. Because one cannot buy Ether on a speculative basis through cryptocurrency exchanges, many investors are more likely to trade the market, which in turn will push the price of Ethereum as it shifts to a mainstream market and catches public interest and media attention. Although the blockchain of Ethereum has been divided into two, the original ETH is still supported by the general public and the core developers.

If you are interested to invest in ether, you should not do it to gain fast cash. It should be that you believe in the project's viability and its potential role in the future of financial services. Take note that as more of Ethereum's blockchains are used in generating smart contracts and decentralized applications, the higher the price of Ether will be.

But just like any other form of investment, there are also several risks involved when purchasing Ether as a speculative form of cryptocurrency.

First, the network used by Ethereum is vulnerable to cyber attacks as proven by what happened during the DOA theft in June. Second, the Ether supply is not fixed and the restraints on the supply in the future are still not certain. The price of any asset could be driven by supply and demand. Therefore, there is always the uncertainty of the assets creating significant risk for investors. Third, EH is not a conventional currency, so you cannot use it to purchase any product or service. Its value is dependent on the viability of Ethereum. Fourth, there is always the risk of the Ethereum network being replaced by a more advanced blockchain technology with similar features. This could eventually lead to a value crash with very low possibility of recovery.

Conclusion

Investing in ETH is like investing in the future of blockchain and cryptocurrency. You have to put your trust into the fact that this technology could impact the way we live.

Chapter 6 - Smart Contracts: Their Impact in Real Life

The primary purpose of creating smart contracts is to allow people to exchange products and services with anyone, often through the web, without going through a centralized organization to serve as third-party middleman.

In smart contracts, several types of contractual clauses could be added to be fully or partially executory. Smart contracts aim to add security to conventional contracts and to minimize the costs of transactions associated with entering into agreements and contracts.

Smart Contracts and Blockchain Technology

Blockchains are primarily based on codes. Although the original blockchains were created to execute minimal and basic operations–primarily transactions for currencies–there are now strategies to let blockchain perform more complicated operations that are defined in basic programs.

The programs run on blockchain, so these carry special features in comparison with other kinds of software. Basically, the program is stored within the network, providing both permanence and resistance to censorship. On top of that, the program is also able to control the blockchain assets so it could store and move currencies. And because the code is performed by the framework, it will consistently behave as written, so no one could disrupt the operation.

In the viewpoint of developers and those directly working on blockchain technology, smart contracts are more often used as reference to the blockchain code. In fact, the term has been specifically linked with the Ethereum platform, whose main purpose is to be a system for performing smart contracts.

Referring to these programs as contracts can actually shift the view for smart contracts as it will show that the platform is guarding valuable transactions. People usually exert effort entering into a contract if it's crucial that the terms should be enforced. In the same vein, we are only using the smart contract code if we have to protect something critical such as identity or money.

In this reference, there's no need for a smart contract to resemble anything that we will regularly refer to as a contract. Even though the code can spell out a conditional transaction for money exchanges, it can also be a governing platform that can regulate account verifications.

In most cases, smart contracts are not used as an isolated system but as a minimal portion of a bigger application. Each blockchain-based app is designed using smart contract to perform operations on their selected blockchain.

Criticisms About Smart Contracts

Criticisms against using smart contracts are somehow valid. Relying on a contract's description can be misleading, because it only highlights one use of the technology. Referring to it as a contract actually fails to capture an important capability of blockchain technology – that this is independent and resistant to censorship.

Essentially, smart contract codes can themselves store cryptocurrency balances, or even regulate other codes for smart contract. After generating smart contracts, the code can move independently when triggered to do a specific act. Hence, most people propose to call them as smart agent, which is similar to the basic idea of a software agent.

As the blockchain technology matures, the reference to smart code as a contract may eventually fade. In the future, we may just refer to a certain language or platform that we are working with, contrary to using a generic term, which could define any complex operation on a blockchain.

Smart Legal Contracts

The term "smart contract" has different interpretations for those working in the financial and legal industry. In this circle, smart contract refers to a certain use of smart code to replace or support current legal contracts.

Most likely, smart legal contracts are made of smart codes and conventional legalese. For example, let's say you have entered into a contract to buy goods from a specific supplier. The payment terms could be stipulated within the code and automatically executed once delivery has been made. However, the retailer may insist that the contract covers indemnity, wherein the supplier is bound to indemnify the retailer against the claims if there are product flaws. It's not practical to represent this in code, because this is not something that could be automatically executed. The clause is open for interpretation and will only be enforced by a court after a litigation proceeding.

Agreements in commercial exchanges are filled with clauses that are included to protect parties from different liabilities, and these are not always ideal for execution and representation through code, meaning that smart legal contracts may need integration of natural language and code.

Are smart legal contracts enforceable by law? This is possible. Take note that the conditions under which the agreement becomes enforceable are flexible and could be suited to the basic relationship between the parties, and do not depend on the form that the contract takes. Remember that an obligation exists if there is a meeting of the mind. Anything from an oral agreement to an informal email thread could become an enforceable contract, if the basic elements are present.

Different kinds of contracts exist around the world, but only some can be used as "smart contracts". In real-life setting, a legal contract can be anything from an oral agreement for someone to clean the yard to a currency traded digitally in forex markets.

Since recently, the use cases getting the most attention are smart legal contracts in smart financial instruments such as bonds, shares, or derivatives. Specifying these contracts in blockchains will allow financial markets to become automated and make the process easier for trading and servicing financial instruments.

Financial instruments are just one form of contract, which can benefit from blockchain technology. As the technology progresses, other assets such as real estate or intellectual property could be stored and exchanged over blockchain frameworks. As new kinds of assets become on-chain, the agreements utilized to govern these assets (such as licensing and mortgage) could take advantage of blockchain analogs.

Smart Contracts as Alternatives to Traditional Legal Contracts

Most advocates for blockchain are seeing more possibilities. Instead of simply imitating or complementing legal contracts that we use today, possibly smart contract code can be used to perform new forms of commercial contracts.

We may even call this an alternative term using smart codes to generate novel, alternate types of agreements, which are nevertheless useful in commerce. Some call this as smart alternative contracts.

This methodology takes a general view of problems in the real-world setting solved by contracts. Remember, the economy relies on every unit (individuals and businesses) to create stable and projectable contracts with one another. Agreements, along with a robust legal system, are the main mechanisms we use to form every incentives for the party to the point where they have enough confidence in their connection for engagement in business and trade that is filled with risks.

However, there is also the viewpoint that legal agreements are not the only solution for this concern. Smart contract codes provide a new set of tools to specify and enforce terms, and these could be used to generate systems of rewards, which could be sufficient to facilitate trade relationships.

The most popular opportunity for this kind is machine-to-machine trade. The expanding framework of smart devices–specifically those independent to an extent–could eventually need a way to deal in basic trade relationships with each other. For example, a refrigerator that purchases food supplies for the family or a coffee maker that orders coffee online if supply runs low.

These processes still need a minimum level of trust to become commercially feasible, but are not suitable for legal agreements that are comparatively costly and need the engagement of legal entities such as a business or people. Still, alternative contracts may enable a whole new form of commerce carried out between cars, computers, mobile phones, and gadgets.

Conclusion

Smart legal contracts are so new that they have minimal effects on real-life settings. Basically, the lack of clear definition in this field is still a sad reality. If you are working in the blockchain field, you should be mindful of how the term is used in various communities. The various uses of the term shows a wide range of concerns in the blockchain field.

Blockchain developers are excited about the endless possibilities of software without sometimes looking into the subtleties and trade practicalities signified in conventional legal contracts. Lawyers, on the other hand, usually look at smart contracts and perceive marginally improved legal agreements without understanding the fuller potential of blockchain to reach beyond legalese.

Chapter 7 - Examples of Blockchains Applications

The blockchain industry is still in its infancy, so it is not yet mainstream. But based on reports, there are about $1 billion investments in blockchain, especially in Financial Technology or Fintech.

In this Chapter, we will take a peek on three of the most successful startups at the moment. Ethereum is a very successful blockchain startup but we have already discussed this company in Chapter 5, so we have excluded it here.

Successful Blockchain Startups Today

Blockstream

Blockstream is a startup which works on accelerating the progress of open assets, cryptocurrency, and smart contracts – all are based on the blockchain platform. The company is behind the blockchain product known as Liquid, which is targeted at hastening the transfer times between trading bitcoins.

The company has already announced Series A funding, hoping to raise $55 million that will be used to boost the startup's protocol and raise these technologies to the nest stage. The company also forged a partnership with PwC to further study blockchain technology as well as assess the sidechain advantages within the fintech world.

A flagship project for Blockstream is known as the Lightning Network – a new platform that can shift smaller BTC transactions off the blockchain so they can be completed faster and further reduce fees.

Through the Lightning Network, the total number of transactions to be settled on the BTC blockchain can be reduced. This also brings down the total number of blocks in the chain.

However, the startup faced several technical challenges before going live. This includes the different changes to the Bitcoin Core. But still, the startup resolved the issues and the Lightning Network is posed to relieve the present accumulation of blocks in the BTC framework. This will also increase the robustness of the BTC framework.

Augur

Augur is a blockchain startup that is offering a projection market platform, and is often regarded as the future of forecasting. Through Augur, you can place custom bets and trade actual money around the world by leveraging on the decentralized framework of Ethereum. The Augur code is residing in the blockchain system of Ethereum, so no one could close the code down, in contrary to the conventional products that could be subject to different legal and regulatory limits in specific jurisdictions.

What is really fascinating about Augur is that it cannot be regulated by any person or organization, nor will it be shut off by any computer system. Augur mainly uses cryptocurrencies so there are no banks or credit card companies involved. Even if the platform run against certain regulations, there's no established company to sue, no servers to take off, and no CEO to be sent to jail.

During the crowdsale of Augur, about $5.3 million was raised for the startup's Reputation or REP tokens in form of ETH 1.1 or BTC 19,000. About 4,800 accounts joined in the sale, which equates to an average purchase of $1100. It is interesting to note that about $600k was invested by Joe Castello – a successful entrepreneur who was once considered to be the next Apple CEO.

Lisk

Lisk offers a decentralized application platform that is similar to Ethereum, but it runs on Sidechains and is written in JavaScript. The company has recently completed its crowdfunding and has already raised about BTC 14,000 or more than $5.7 Million.

Lisk offers an alternative application platform to other decentralized frameworks due to its simplicity. And because it is coded on JavaScript, programmers can also create their own dapps with ease.

The Lisk team also collaborated with Microsoft so its decentralized app platform could be used in the Azure cloud. Microsoft has already integrated Lisk into its own blockchain as a BaaS, which means that developers around the world can develop, test, and use Lisk centralized applications using the Azure cloud computing infrastructure and platform.

The platform will let JavaScript developers follow this by providing them the required tools to use the blockchain app as a sidechain on the Lisk network. They also don't have to learn complicated languages for every blockchain used.

Through Lisk, anyone can code, deploy, and use their decentralized applications in a fast and safe way over the Lisk network.

This February 2016, the company raised about $5.8 million in the form of bitcoins and other blockchain assets.

Chapter 8 - Future Developments in Big Financial Industries

In the current model for banks and other financial services firms, a centralized ledger serves as the keeper of transactions. But as we have discussed in the previous chapters, the blockchain platform is decentralized. The information is publicly accessible on a cloud-based server. There is no central organization that serves as the third-party or middleman. This absence of unified authority is the key factor that disrupts the present banking models.

Visionaries in financial technology believe that blockchain is the next stage in the evolution of trade, and it is obvious to see how it can change how we buy and sell products and services. The capacity of modern technology to provide a secured storage of identity, covering even the record of transactions of an individual, is an area that is now being explored in the financial world.

We are now in the era of fast-paced revolution as the banking industry is further exploring financial technology, specifically blockchain and how it could affect their business frameworks.

But the big banks are not only the players in this evolution. Hundreds of startups are working to take advantage of blockchain. The conventional viewpoint about the significance of traditional banks is being questioned, as there is a notion that a digital system can provide better and cheaper financial services. Conventional business models are now becoming outdated. Blockchain is currently conjuring its magic – growing and evolving without the need for unified regulation.

The Rise of Decentralized Domains

Experts believe that eventually, blockchain can be used to increase the security as well as the speed of transactions between big banks and global companies. But the potential effect of blockchain is not restricted to the big players. It can even change the way every person lives.

Let's take a look at a possible scenario in the future, which can happen real soon.

Adam purchases a brand new car, a condo unit, a smart watch, an iPhone. The things that he has purchased have serial numbers on them for identification and are embedded with chips so they can be connected to the web (remember IoT?).

Upon buying the products, each is recorded under Adam's name using his digital identification (could be biometric or similar technology). The storage of this transaction occurs within a blockchain framework.

Now, Adam has several devices that are able to transact on his behalf – his car, his apartment, his smart watch, his iPhone. His car initiates auto-refueling as it navigates the highways. His apartment reorders every needed supply. His smart watch can connect with the apartment to prepare the house for the master's arrival.

Every transaction is considered as a purchase around Adam's wallet, but it involves no verification. Verification is already taken care of because the system recognizes the devices involved.

For bigger transactions, or probably just to check once in a while (similar to digital payments today), Adam is requested to agree that his device is ordering items online by touching his iPhone's screen to scan his thumb for biometric signals. All these things occurred and are monitored on the public ledger within a blockchain network maintained by the bank for easy, affordable, and accessible purchases.

The future will be cashless. Big banks can leverage on this through blockchain.

The reason why we will be devoid of printed money in the near future is that our transactions could be facilitated digitally around use, through blockchain and IoT.

You shop in a store, and your phone will communicate your location and your behavior. In fact, Amazon stores is set to roll out its stores in 2017. These stores have no checkout counters and cashiers as you can purchase items through your phone and you will be charged in your Amazon account.

You don't have to pay anything. You just need to verify the transaction in milliseconds.

According to experts, by year 2030, the only people who are still using cash or credit cards are those willing to pay the extra costs charged by banks and merchants for their transactions. Most people will adopt the chip-based transactions facilitated by blockchain technology.

Conclusion

You should now have a good understanding of blockchain, how it works, and its potential to disrupt current industries and change the future of society. Consider everything you have learned as you plan your next move. Is it finally time to invest in this emerging advancement? Would it be best to join the revolution, regardless of the risks? Or, should you wait a bit longer despite the possibility of reaping smaller rewards?

Regardless of your choice, know that the future may already be here, and it's up to you to take advantage of the opportunities it brings.

www.ingramcontent.com/pod-product-compliance
Lightning Source LLC
Chambersburg PA
CBHW061146180526
45170CB00002B/645